Asperger syndrome – practical strategies for the classroom

A teacher's guide

AUTHORS

Leicester City Council Education Department

Autism Outreach Service

George Thomas

Leicestershire County Council Education Department

Autism Outreach Team

Penny Barratt

Heather Clewley

Helen Joy

Mo Potter

Educational Psychology Service

Philip Whitaker

THE NATIONAL
AUTISTIC SOCIETY

AAPC

Kelly Sharitt
683 - 9381

Acknowledgements

This booklet was produced by the authors during the course of their work for Leicester City Council and Leicestershire County Council. It is based on their work in supporting youngsters with Asperger syndrome in mainstream schools.

We would like to thank the parents of the local Asperger Syndrome Support group who highlighted the need to raise awareness and provide guidance for mainstream schools. Our thanks also to classroom staff for their help in developing and testing many of these strategies.

First published 1998 by
The National Autistic Society
393 City Road
London EC1V 1NE

ISBN 1-931282-08-0

Designed by Cottier & Sidaway Design Partnership

The Autism Asperger Publishing Company is proud to be the sole U.S. publisher of this book and a series of other carefully selected books on autism spectrum disorders originally published by the National Autistic Society (NAS) of Great Britain. To be faithful to the authors, we have maintained the British spellings, punctuations, etc. We have, however, provided a list of the American equivalents in an effort to provide the most relevant and useful information to our readers.

Other NAS titles published by AAPC include:
- *Asperger Syndrome - Practical Strategies for the Classroom: A Teacher's Guide* by Leicester City Council and Leicestershire County Council
- *Challenging Behaviour and Autism: Making Sense - Making Progress: A Guide to Preventing and Managing Challenging Behaviour for Parents and Teachers* by Philip Whitaker
- *Everybody is Different: A Book for Young People Who Have Brothers or Sisters with Autism* by Fiona Bleach
- *It Can Get Better ... Dealing with Common Behaviours Problems in Young Autistic Children: A Guide to Caregivers* by Paul Dickinson and Liz Hannah
- *Teaching Young Children with Autistic Spectrum Disorders to Learn: A Practical Guide for Parents and Staff in General Education Classrooms and Preschools* by Liz Hannah
- *What is Asperger Syndrome and How Will it Affect Me? A Guide for Young People* by Martine Ives of the Autism Helpline

List of Great Britain terms and their U.S. equivalents

fire bell - fire alarm
Head Teacher - principal
holiday - vacation
homework diary - assignment planner
lesson - class
residential trip - field trip
secondary school - middle/high school
timetable - schedule

Contents

An introduction to this guide

Although individuals with a diagnosis of Asperger syndrome may differ greatly from each other, all share a common cluster of underlying difficulties. In this guide we outline the nature of the underlying impairments, explain how these may give rise to problems in school, and provide practical management suggestions.

The first part of the guide gives an overview of Asperger syndrome and outlines the three core areas of impairment. In this section we also comment briefly on educational provision for pupils with Asperger syndrome. The remainder of the guide is broken down into six sections, three corresponding to the 'core' impairments and a further three focused on broad areas of difficulty which are commonly experienced or presented in school.

The guide is not intended to be read from cover to cover and we have adopted a common format to help readers identify the pages which are of most relevance. The features of this format are as follows:

- a title which identifies the specific topic
- a brief case 'vignette' to help you decide if what follows will apply to the youngster you have in mind
- **'Making sense of it'** tries to shed light on the way in which the core impairments may be contributing to that particular problem.
- **'Things to try'** identifies strategies and practical tips drawn from our experience. Although they may not precisely fit your situation or the youngster with whom you are working, we hope our suggestions will get you thinking along the right lines.

Throughout, our aim has been to help you make sense of the difficulties which the youngster with Asperger syndrome may experience and present. In our experience, this is a vital foundation for putting into practice the sort of practical strategies which we outline.

An introduction to Asperger syndrome

Asperger syndrome is generally regarded as a form of autism and is named after the German psychiatrist who first described the condition in the 1940s. The children Asperger worked with all had significant difficulties affecting the way they related to and communicated with others.

A triad of impairments

People with Asperger syndrome have problems in the areas of **social interaction, communication, and lack of flexibility of thought** – they may lack imagination, may have very intense or narrow interests and may be very fond of routine. For a diagnosis to be made, specific types and degrees of impairment must be present in each of these three areas (usually referred to as the triad of impairments). Having said this, however, it should be emphasised that there is a good deal of variation in the overall severity of the difficulties experienced, and the way in which the difficulties show themselves will vary. It should also be stressed that every person with Asperger syndrome has a unique personality which has been shaped by individual life experiences (just as we all have).

Like autism, Asperger syndrome is the result of an organic problem, and not caused by the way a child is brought up. Unlike people with autism, those with Asperger syndrome have fewer problems with language development and are less likely to have additional learning difficulties. The physiological basis of autism and Asperger syndrome is still not clearly understood.

Key features of Asperger syndrome

Interaction and social relationships

Some children with Asperger syndrome may appear to prefer their own company. They may have an acute awareness of their personal space, showing signs of feeling uncomfortable if others come too near. Many try hard to be sociable but when they approach others they seem to be socially clumsy. They may not look at the person whom they are approaching, or they may inadvertently give the 'wrong signals'. They may compensate for their difficulties by being over formal. They have great problems in picking up cues about what is expected in particular situations: they may behave with a Headteacher in just the same way as they do with their friends or parents. They are also likely to have problems handling confrontations and may unwittingly behave in antisocial ways.

Communication

Despite having a well developed vocabulary and grammar, children with Asperger syndrome have an impaired understanding of what communication is all about. They may be unaware of how to ask for help or when to assert themselves. They may speak in a monotonous voice, with poor control of volume or intonation. Much of their talk may centre on a preferred subject to which they return again and again with an almost obsessive monotony. They may have trouble understanding jokes, idiom and metaphor. Their language can appear rather stilted or pedantic. The quality of their communication will deteriorate sharply under stress. Lack of facial expression, limited gesture and poor judgement of other people's body language also contributes to their communication difficulties.

Imagination and inflexibility of thinking

Children with Asperger syndrome characteristically have limited play skills. They tend to prefer mechanical activities such as collecting, assembling or dismantling. They may learn to play pretend games, but later than their normally developing peers. Where such play is learned, it is often rather repetitious. Other elements of this lack of flexible thinking include a dislike of change, a preference for sameness and the development of routines and rituals.

It is common for people with Asperger syndrome to develop very strong interests in rather narrow and unusual areas. Individuals with Asperger syndrome also have problems 'putting themselves in other people's shoes', or seeing things from a different point of view. They feel happiest when they only have to deal with the concrete and predictable.

Additional difficulties

Problems with motor skills and unusual responses to sensory stimuli are also common in youngsters with Asperger syndrome. These, together with the core impairments, can contribute to a range of significant difficulties, particularly in terms of work skills and emotional vulnerability.

Strengths

Despite difficulties in dealing with the social domain, children with Asperger syndrome may well have considerable strengths. They may have: an unusually good rote memory; extraordinarily focused, if narrow, interests; an extensive vocabulary; advanced knowledge or skills in areas of technology or science.

Educational provision for children with Asperger syndrome

As we have emphasised, there is a very wide range of variation in the severity of the difficulties experienced by people diagnosed as having Asperger syndrome. The way in which the so-called 'core impairments' are manifested will also vary a good deal. Because there is a spectrum of need, so there has to be a corresponding spectrum of provision. In catering for such children the following points and principles need to be noted:

- Successful work tends to be a mixture of enhancing skills (particularly in the key areas of impairment) and adapting the environment.
- Support should be based on need (rather than diagnosis).
- Schools need to respond within the framework of the Individuals with Disabilities Act (just as for any other form of special educational need).

In practice, almost all youngsters with Asperger syndrome are in general education classrooms. Some have support within this setting and others may receive services in a resource room. A few may require a more restrictive setting such as a self-contained classroom.

What if I think a child may have Asperger syndrome?

If you think a child has Asperger Syndrome, you should discuss this matter with the child's parents and your special education coordinator. The child's parents might seek a referral to a psychiatrist as well as meet with the special education multidisciplinary team.

Social relationships

Joining in and making friends

"Graham tries to join in and make friends – but all he seems to do is get on other people's nerves. No-one wants to spend any time with him."

Making sense of it

- People with Asperger syndrome often want the friendship of others but do not understand how to go about making friends.
- It can be very difficult for some to pick up the social cues that invite social interaction.
- When trying to make conversation the person with Asperger syndrome may not read the non-verbal signals which are involved in turn-taking. They may not appreciate the clues which the listener is giving about the relevance and interest of the chosen topic. The person with Asperger syndrome may talk **at** the listener endlessly and in excessive detail about obscure subjects.
- Some people with Asperger syndrome may stand too close, use non-verbal signals in an awkward or poorly timed way and may speak in a rather monotonous tone of voice.
- Some may have difficulty in getting the level of familiarity right. They may be excessively formal or conversely treat a virtual stranger as if he or she were an intimate friend.

Things to try

- Graham may need to be explicitly taught rules and conventions which most people pick up intuitively. Examples might include how to greet people, ways of handing over or ending a conversation, how to tell if the other person is interested.
- If Graham goes on and on about a specific topic, definite limits should be set on when the topic can and cannot be introduced into conversation. A clear signal may be used to remind Graham. This could be a gesture or a 'code' word or phrase.
- Graham may need to have normal conversational styles modelled for him, with feedback which helps raise awareness of particular strategies and conventions. A framework such as that provided in *The Social Use of Language* (Rinaldi, NFER) may be helpful in breaking down the skills of conversation into manageable targets. It is worth remembering that the didactic style most often used by teachers when talking to a whole class is not actually a very good model for conversation.

- It is important to promote the tolerance and understanding of others in the class towards Graham. Encourage other children to approach him, perhaps in the context of structured classroom activities.
- Exposure to less structured contact with classmates may need to be reduced. Graham may function better in formal activities with some degree of structure (eg clubs involving organised recreational or educational activities).
- Involving younger children in organised playground games is a way of increasing levels of social contact while providing a degree of structure.

Coping with groups

"At playtime all Ranjit seems to do is wander about on his own. In the classroom he can't bear to be the centre of attention."

Making sense of it

- Youngsters with Asperger syndrome often feel lost or confused by free time. Break and lunchtime can be particularly stressful given the informality and low level of structure in these situations. This may lead them to opt out.
- Some may have difficulty making sense of the unwritten and flexible rules that usually govern playground activities. They also have problems in understanding the 'rules' about how people relate to each other.
- Even in one to one situations some find the demands of relating to other people too difficult to deal with and will seek to avoid or minimise contact.
- Where contact cannot be avoided they may try to control the interaction by sticking to very rigid routines or specific topics of conversation.
- Work in less structured group situations or simply having to sit close to a large group of other children can be a very difficult and anxious experience for some pupils with Asperger syndrome.
- Avoidance of others may be the result of bullying. Some are particularly vulnerable to teasing and bullying.
- Such children may be able to cope with classroom routines but have great difficulty if they are asked to make a contribution in a less familiar activity.

Things to try

- If you feel that break time is too confusing or upsetting it may be best initially to find ways of providing more structure or occupying Ranjit with some other activity.
- Raising awareness of Ranjit's difficulties and building some support among his peers can create a more relaxed and tolerant environment. It may be possible to set up informal buddy systems or even use the peer group to help teach a range of coping strategies. 'Circles of Friends' (see **Further Reading – p49**) are one form of support that can benefit both the student with Asperger syndrome and his or her school mates.
- Ranjit may need to be 'de-sensitised' to group activities. This involves **gradually** requiring his involvement in activities which involve him in higher levels of contact. To begin with the emphasis may need to be only on tolerating physical proximity. It may then be possible to work on raising levels of contact and co-operation. High levels of structure and explicit rules are always likely to be needed to guide co-operative activities. Youngsters like Ranjit will have extreme difficulty with the sort of intuitive negotiation and shared understanding of 'fairness' etc which operate in such situations.
- Remember, as well, that some youngsters do not want to make friends or spend all their time in other people's company. This needs to be respected.

Making sense of people

"David can't tell when people are just joking. He doesn't realise when teachers are really cross with him. He just doesn't seem to 'read' people."

Making sense of it

- When we talk to someone we rely on a range of non-verbal signals, such as facial expression, body language and eye contact to get our message across. People with Asperger syndrome have trouble working out the meaning of these signals.
- Some people with Asperger syndrome may find it easier to listen and understand if they block out the non-verbal signals (for example, by not looking at the speaker). They are likely to either not understand or misinterpret these non-verbal signals.
- Some may experience great difficulty in 'putting themselves in other people's shoes'. It might be very hard for them to grasp what another person is thinking or feeling: they may not understand why a person might be saying something "just for fun".
- Sharing a joke with others is often a way to get accepted socially. The person with Asperger syndrome may have great difficulty in coping with the double meanings that are essential parts of humour.
- As a way of dealing with these difficulties in understanding others some may try to impose very rigid rules or routines on situations.

Things to try

- Try to speak as calmly and clearly as possible if there have been problems. The raised voice, animated expressions and forceful gestures which we tend to use instinctively can get in the way of David understanding. He may be overloaded or alarmed by all this extra information and it may distract him from the point you are really trying to get across.
- It is important not to rely on David reading 'between the lines'. You may need to explain exactly what you mean, particularly when it involves behaviour in social situations.
- You may need to teach David about specific situations, such as how to tell if someone is joking (as opposed to bullying); how another person might be feeling in specific situations; how to tell if someone has done something 'on purpose' (rather than by accident). David will probably always have to work this sort of thing out logically or 'by the rules' – rather than sensing them intuitively like most of us do.
- David may be helped by games and role play activities which involve him in thinking about another person's viewpoint. Progress may be slow and unpredictable and it is always important to spell out how such experiences might apply to his day to day life.
- It may be necessary to teach particular behaviours to deal with specific situations (eg how to behave when someone is cross with you). David may always find it difficult to respond intuitively or 'naturally', but he can be taught what to do to prevent him from making things worse. In effect, you will be aiming to provide a simple 'script'.

When friendships fail

"Tom gets so cross and frustrated with other people – and then he just lashes out."

Making sense of it

- People with Asperger syndrome are often acutely aware of their own difficulties and may be desperate to make friends (see **Emotional difficulties – Self awareness – p39**).
- They may see others talking but not grasp the informal understandings that underlie much social 'chat'. This can be very frustrating.
- The problem may become more acute in adolescence when friendships are increasingly based on mutual empathy and shared understanding.
- Continual, unsuccessful attempts to make friends and continuing demands to deal with people can be very stressful to the person with Asperger syndrome. This may lead to aggressive behaviour.
- Individuals with Asperger syndrome often show little awareness of their own feelings (just as they are unaware of the feelings of others). Even if they do recognise their own feelings they may not realise that others might be interested and able to help.

Things to try

- Tom needs to be helped to sense warning signs within himself and to anticipate problem situations. It may be helpful for him to have a 'script' or list of things to do when he is becoming upset or stressed. You may need to go as far as to write these down so that they can be carried round. They can consist of either strategies to calm himself down or arrangements which allow him to remove himself from the situation. He will need to be prompted and encouraged to use these scripts.
- It is vital to work with Tom's classmates to help them make sense of his difficulties. Classmates can also be involved in informal buddy systems or more formal approaches such as 'Circles of Friends' (see **Further Reading – p49**). Such approaches can help promote Tom's acceptance. Peers can also tutor and model specific skills.
- It may help Tom to have a regular, set opportunity to get support from a particular member of staff. He may also benefit from the opportunity to tell his side of the story.
- Remember not to forget 'everyday' strategies such as incentive (and disincentive) systems. Youngsters like Tom benefit from 'rules' being made very explicit and specific and from linking these to concrete rewards.

Interrupting

"William interrupts me all the time. It happens when I'm talking to the group and even when I'm talking to just one other person."

Making sense of it

- People with Asperger syndrome can have serious difficulty in knowing how and when to join conversations. They may not recognise the pauses and subtle signals which invite them to join in the conversation.
- They may lack the skills of commenting or building on the contribution of another speaker, as a way of joining in the conversation.
- People with Asperger syndrome may become so pre-occupied with a particular thought or topic that they cannot resist blurting it out.

Things to try

- In group situations try using an object such as a stone or bean bag with only the person holding the object being allowed to speak.
- You may need to explain to William that pauses in conversation are the places to come in with his comments. He may need to practice recognising pauses. Videos of television programmes might be useful for this.
- If William continues to have serious difficulty in recognising when and how to join in, then you may need to devise an agreed signal, to be used by supportive adults or peers.

Appearing rude

"Jordan often appears rude to other people. He talks as though he is an adult telling the other children off."

Making sense of it

- Children with Asperger syndrome may learn their language skills by copying 'chunks' of language which they hear. This copying will include not just the adult's language but also their intonation and the 'attitude' they may have adopted when they said these words.
- Many people with Asperger syndrome lack an intuitive understanding of social rules and expectations in particular situations – they may treat adults just like classmates and vice-versa.

Things to try

- It may be useful to use a Circle of Friends (or similar) as a forum in which peers can tell Jordan how his language affects them.
- Jordan will need opportunities to observe how his peers speak and interact with others. He should then be helped to rehearse and try out strategies based on these models. Video could be used, if Jordan finds the 'live' situations too stressful.
- It may be helpful to show Jordan videos of himself interacting inappropriately, highlighting what would be appropriate behaviour and role playing this. (This will need to be handled sensitively so as not to damage Jordan's self esteem.)

Communication

Not responding to instructions

"Sula appears to be listening when an adult gives instructions to a group of children, but she then can't do what she's been told without copying the others."

Making sense of it

- Some people with Asperger syndrome cannot take in group instructions, perhaps not understanding that they are one of the group and that the instruction is meant for them as well as for the other children.
- Some have found ways of **appearing** to listen. This skill avoids them being singled out.
- Some have poor receptive skills. This means that they may not understand the language the adult is using when addressing the whole group. See **Understanding adult language – p18**
- Some people with Asperger syndrome develop alternative, coping strategies when unable to follow group instructions. A very common coping strategy is to copy what the other children do: this may mask serious comprehension problems.
- Poor motivation may mean that these youngsters do not put in the extra effort which is needed for them to listen to and process instructions.

Things to try

- Sula may need the group instructions repeating to her individually. This could be done by (a) an adult who has the task of supporting Sula; (b) the person who gave the group instruction; or (c) a peer. It is important that Sula learns to respond to a range of people doing this for her (See **Work skills – Over-dependency – p44**).
- It may be sufficient for the adult giving the instruction to mention Sula's name before giving the instruction so that she knows she is included in the 'group'.
- Check out, in informal situations, whether Sula does understand the type of language used in group situations. If she doesn't, consider lowering the language level, using shorter sentences with key words and not using difficult and complex sentences. This is likely to benefit other people in the group, as well as Sula.
- Coping strategies, such as observing other people's response to a group instruction, should be encouraged in conjunction with the other strategies suggested above.

Understanding adult language

*"David seems very bright and he's got an excellent vocabulary –
but when I explain something in class he doesn't seem to
have a clue."*

Making sense of it

- Children with Asperger syndrome often have good memories (particularly for facts) and can acquire extensive vocabularies. This may lead people to over-estimate their understanding of language and particularly their ability to cope with abstract concepts. In fact, they are often very concrete in their thinking and understanding of language.
- Attending to instructions or explanations in group settings seems particularly difficult. They may not be 'tuning into' the relevant aspects of what's going on or may be distracted by inessential details.
- The longer the explanation or instruction and the more abstract the underlying ideas, the more difficult it is for children with Asperger syndrome.
- The person with Asperger syndrome often has a very concrete and literal understanding of language. Idiosyncratic speech, metaphors and uses of language such as sarcasm or jokes may be interpreted literally.
- The social difficulties experienced by children with Asperger syndrome may also affect their understanding of language. Even if they understand the actual words they may not be able to grasp the speaker's underlying meaning or intentions. This is a particular problem with language such as sarcasm where people may say one thing with their speech and another with their non-verbal signals. This makes children with Asperger syndrome very vulnerable to teasing.
- These difficulties are often at their worst when behaviour problems are being dealt with. The added emotion and non-verbal signals which are instinctively used by the adult can obscure the point that is being made.

Things to try

- Get David's attention **before** you speak to him (particularly if giving specific instructions). In group situations position him as close to you as possible and prompt (and reward) attention. Use his name **before** you give an instruction.
- It may help to use something that interests him to gain and motivate his attention, eg "Later on we'll be talking about clocks, but first I want you to ..."
- Think about how to organise your explanations and instructions:
    - it is helpful to summarise the main points in advance (and even provide a list)
    - give 'advance warning' as you get to main points
    - repeat and summarise
    - try to organise and chunk information into coherent sections
    - try to be explicit about any links you want the child to make to his/her everyday knowledge on topics covered in schools.
- Try to monitor your pace of speaking and do build in pauses to allow 'processing time'.

- Youngsters like David will be helped by visual cues. Some information and concepts can be represented in pictorial form or at a more advanced stage in the form of diagrams and key words.

- Though it is a difficult challenge, try to keep your language as simple as possible. Use short direct sentences with explicit links between ideas. Be prepared to re-phrase if necessary.

- If specialist or abstract/non-literal language is going to be used, try to explain it separately, before David meets it in his work.

- David also needs to do his bit. It is particularly important that he learns to monitor his attention and understanding. He will need to be told exactly what to do if he loses the thread or doesn't understand something. He should be encouraged to ask questions to clarify.

- If you need to deal with any misbehaviour from David try to keep your tone as neutral as possible and your language as simple as you can. Say clearly what you feel he has done wrong, explain the behaviour that you would like to see instead and be clear about consequences. Check he has understood. You may need to be much more direct and concrete than you would normally be. Long explanations about why a particular behaviour was wrong and attempts to reason with the child may be counterproductive.

- Some children with Asperger syndrome can listen and understand better if they don't look at the speaker. The non-verbal signals may confuse or distract. Don't insist on the child looking while you speak (as long as you feel he or she is listening).

- If any ancillary help is available, use the person as an interpreter, particularly for long instructions and explanations.

Literal interpretations

"John takes everything so literally. When he answers the phone and someone says 'is your mum there?' he says 'yes', but doesn't go and tell his mum."

Making sense of it

- It is very common for people with Asperger syndrome to interpret what other people say and mean in a very literal, concrete way.
- Figures of speech (eg 'stretch your legs'), humour and sarcasm may pose particular problems.
- In schools it is very common to use indirect (and polite) forms of speech such as 'Can you put your books away', or 'Would you like to...' – these are actually instructions but may be treated as questions by the person with Asperger syndrome.
- Part of this difficulty is caused by the problems in interpreting the speaker's intentions and motivation – this requires making sense of non-verbal clues and, in part, on being able to put yourself in the speaker's shoes.

Things to try

- It would be impossible to stop using all idioms and colloquialisms and also unnatural. However, it is important to check back on what we have said and re-phrase if necessary, eg "Just give me five minutes" could be re-phrased as "I'll talk to you when I've finished watching this programme at 8 o'clock".
- Particularly when giving important instructions use simple, short and direct sentences. Emphasise what you want rather than don't want (eg "Please be quiet !" as opposed to "I don't want all this noise, thank you").
- Encourage John to monitor his own understanding. Explain what he should do if he doesn't understand.
- Teach John some common idioms and sayings (eg 'line up', 'in a minute' etc).
- John may not understand humour and jokes. Start at the level of humour John is at, eg slapstick, knock knock jokes, but discourage him from using these inappropriately or 'going over the top'.

Under or over use of gesture

"When Richard talks to me he stands stiffly and looks like a soldier, he keeps his arms by his side, speaks in a monotone and uses little facial expression."

Making sense of it

- People with Asperger syndrome have difficulty with all aspects of communication, verbal or non-verbal.
- They often have difficulty in interpreting and reading other peoples' body language and facial expression, as well as using these forms of communication spontaneously and appropriately.
- The non-verbal communication skills we use everyday may need to be specifically learnt by those with Asperger syndrome. It can be difficult for them to learn these skills and use them in a flexible or spontaneous way.

Things to try

- Explain Richard's difficulties to his classmates and encourage them to show more tolerance towards him. Get permission from both Richard and his parents before doing this.
- Use the checklist and teaching suggestions from the *Social Use of Language Programme* (Rinaldi, NFER) to work on specific skills. If you can organise a peer support group such as Circle of Friends they can be used to model and tutor (see **Further Reading – p49**).
- Make a point of showing Richard more appropriate strategies in a natural setting, eg in the playground or during out of school activities.
- If Robert uses too much gesture teach him some simple strategies to help him out, eg keeping his hands in his pockets, holding something in his hand, hooking his thumbs into his belt etc.
- Encourage Richard to take part in as many social activities, outings or groups as possible. Encourage and emphasise his verbal strengths in conversation, and include him in as much as possible.

Talking too loudly or too quickly

"Leon talks in such a loud voice he embarrasses whoever he's talking to."

Making sense of it

- People with Asperger syndrome may have little understanding of what other people are thinking or feeling and so do not understand that their behaviour may embarrass someone they are with.
- People with Asperger syndrome are likely to have difficulty 'reading' non-verbal expressions and body language and may not 'recognise' emotions, such as embarrassment in other people.
- They may not have learned the social 'rules' of communication implicitly, as most people do. They are unlikely to recognise that their social behaviour is out of place and inappropriate.
- The inappropriate volume may be an indicator that the person with Asperger syndrome is anxious in that situation.
- People with Asperger syndrome may talk too quietly, too quickly or too slowly as well as too loudly.

Things to try

- Make sure Leon's hearing is normal.
- Model the 'normal' volume that you would like Leon to use and provide opportunities for him to practice this. Increase the range of situations in which he practices an appropriate volume. Start with those that are easiest for him moving up to those in which he has most difficulty controlling his volume.
- Use a cue, such as a gesture, which lets Leon know that he is talking too loudly.
- Use a tape recorder or video to record Leon. Play him the recording, asking him to evaluate his volume. Use this technique sensitively so as not to lower Leon's self esteem.
- Reward Leon for talking at an appropriate volume.

Repetitive questioning

"Jeremy asks the same question over and over for weeks. When he doesn't get the answer he wants, he gets very angry until he does."

Making sense of it

- Some youngsters with Asperger syndrome are extremely rigid in their conversations and enjoy hearing the same answer over and over again, eg "When do the street lights go on ?", wanting the response "When it gets dark", and being extremely upset if an alternative answer is given such as "When it's night time".
- Some may use repetitive questioning in order to 'hold the floor' or keep someone engaged in conversation with them: they may lack the skills to handle the conversation in a more natural way.
- For some people with Asperger syndrome asking repetitive questions can relieve anxiety especially when the questions are concerned with what is going to happen throughout the day.

Things to try

- To begin with, respect Jeremy's attempt at communication and give him time to ask his questions when he needs to. This may act as a 'calming' strategy and allow him to engage in more purposeful communication later.
- Offer and teach Jeremy how to use more appropriate calming strategies, eg listening to music on a walkman, outside the school setting, reading a favourite book, using a stress-relief toy or whatever might be appropriate.
- Provide visual information such as a timetable which lets Jeremy know what is going to happen during the day, so that he doesn't need to keep asking.
- Gradually change or 'shape' your reply to the obsessive questions. For example, to the question "Can I go now?" that has to be replied "Yes you may", accompany the reply with a nod or thumbs up, gradually reducing the verbal reply so that just a gesture will do.
- Use Jeremy's repetitive questioning as a learning opportunity. Tell him you will answer his question when he has complied with a request from you.
- Gradually ration the time you will respond to his repetitive questioning, eg "I can't answer you now, but I can talk to you at 11 o'clock for five minutes". It is important to ensure that you do as you have said.
- Only allow repetitive questioning in one particular place, eg the playground. It is important that he has access to this place several times a day.
- Be explicit in limiting the questioning but invite more appropriate conversation, "This question is boring, but ask me something else" (or "talk to me about ..."). Also see **Obsessive topics of conversation – p25.**

Imagination/ rigidity

"It's so difficult to have a chat with Michael, he just goes on and on about clocks. It's so boring !"

Making sense of it
- Talking about an obsessional interest to the exclusion of other topics and without regard to the listener's interest is a common feature of people with Asperger syndrome.
- This sort of obsession may serve the function of reducing anxiety – just like other forms of ritual do.
- Alternatively Michael may be doing this because he actually wants to engage in conversation – but doesn't know how to 'chat'.

Things to try
- It is important to understand his reasons for going on and on about this topic – but it is important to begin to reduce the extent to which it is allowed to intrude on his thoughts and conversations. Identify 'special times' when he can talk about his interests and actively discourage these topics at all other times. Gradually try to reduce the duration and number of these special times.
- Opportunity to talk about his 'pet subject' can also be used as an incentive for completing tasks etc.
- **If** Michael's obsessive talking is a way of coping with anxiety try to find other ways to help him. It may be possible to remove some of the causes of his worry – or you may need to offer him alternative, less intrusive methods of calming himself.
- Make sure you praise Michael and give him attention when he is **not** talking about his interests (even if he only manages this for a short period).
- Try to use his interests in talking about favourite topics as a way of developing conversational knowledge and response to the particular topic.
- Teach Michael when and with who it is appropriate to talk about clocks. You will need to be fairly explicit about this.
- If the obsession is socially appropriate look for opportunities for Michael to talk about his interest with other people who share the same interests.
- With Michael's agreement (and possibly participation) talk with his classmates about how they can tell him clearly when they have had enough of a particular topic (a 'code word' or agreed signal that everyone uses can be helpful).

Insisting on rules

"Yatin follows rules really well. In situations where other children are bending or breaking the rules he'll take on an adult role and tell them off."

Making sense of it

- Explicit rules provide useful boundaries to and guidance for people with Asperger syndrome.
- Due to a difficulty with flexible thought people with Asperger syndrome may not appreciate that there are times and situations where rules can be bent, re-negotiated or broken.
- Some may be unable to see another person's point of view and will be unable to appreciate why they might have not strictly adhered to a rule.
- Children with Asperger syndrome need a sense of order and stability. If rules change or appear 'flexible' they may become anxious. Their only strategy may be one of resorting to an inappropriate adult role.

Things to try

- You need to be aware that Yatin is likely to strictly adhere to any rule. It is therefore important to think carefully about how the rules are worded, building some flexibility into them.
- Because Yatin is going to have difficulty understanding why rules are not always strictly adhered to make sure someone, either an adult or a peer, explains the situation fully to him, particularly explaining why people are doing what they are doing.
- Explain sensitively to Yatin that peers do not appreciate him taking on the adult role of telling them off. Talk with him about alternative ways to express or deal with his concern. Practise these alternatives and prompt their use in appropriate situations.
- Write Yatin a series of 'Social Stories' to explain why people sometimes bend or break rules (see **Further Reading – p49**).

Phobias

"Susan is petrified of dogs. It's got to the point where she won't go outside the house, not even into the garden."

Making sense of it

- People with Asperger syndrome often make very rigid connections, frequently based on a single experience. Some aspect of a situation or experience may have caused them distress in the past – similar situations then trigger exactly the same reactions. The fear may also 'spread' to other, quite different situations.
- As with all phobias, continued avoidance allows fears to grow out of all proportion and the person never learns (for instance) that most dogs are harmless.

Things to try

- It is important to start, wherever possible, to find out what it is about dogs that Susan dislikes, eg their fur, barking, tails etc. This is best achieved by asking Susan herself. Most people with Asperger syndrome can tell us about their fears, but we often forget to ask them. When looked at from Susan's perspective her phobia of dogs may seem rational and understandable. If Susan is unable to tell you about her phobia you can still follow the strategies outlined below in a more general way.
- Once you have understood Susan's phobia you need to set realistic targets. It may not be realistic or necessary for Susan to tolerate physical contact with dogs – but she needs to be able to see them at a distance without panicking.
- Try to desensitise Susan to her phobia. The basic principle of this process is very gradual exposure to the source of her anxiety while simultaneously keeping her relaxed. In practice this may mean involving Susan in some pleasurable activity (such as eating an ice cream or playing with a favourite toy) while playing a tape recording at low volume of a dog barking. Pictures and videos can then be gradually introduced before she encounters the real thing at a distance. It is essential to allow Susan to pace this process and to continue offering pleasurable and relaxing experiences while she is exposed to the source of her fears.
- A 'Social Story' may be helpful in altering Susan's expectations about dogs and teaching her how to react in their presence (see **Further Reading – p49**).

Changing the way things are done

"Hugh likes everything to happen in a set order. If I try to break his routine he gets really upset."

Making sense of it

■ People with Asperger syndrome may have difficulty predicting future events. Because of this, some insist on things happening in a set order. This order provides a sense of security and comfort. A change in routine may threaten this sense of security and hence cause anxiety.

■ Some people with Asperger syndrome seem to have a strong need to complete something, once they have started it. This compulsion seems to take priority over whatever else they should be doing and they may become very upset if unable to 'finish off'.

Things to try

■ Try to gradually reduce the length of time it takes Hugh to get through one of his routines. Start off with one step in the routine. It can be helpful to introduce an artificial signal, such as kitchen timer, to mark the end of the step. Initially this should be set so that the step takes its usual time. Once Hugh comes to expect the signal as part of the routine, set it for shorter and shorter intervals.

■ If the routine seems to have lots of steps and stages, try to miss out the shortest, smallest or apparently least important step. Hugh might find this easier to accept if given a timetable which leaves out the smallest steps (see **Preparing for change – p29**).

■ When Hugh becomes comfortable with the timetable, then you may slowly be able to remove more steps from the routine. At this stage it is also worth introducing slight variations to some of the steps, in order to encourage him to be more tolerant of change.

■ As Hugh may have difficulty predicting, you may find that he will be willing to leave an activity and return to it later, as long as you can reassure him that he will be able to do so. You may need to show him on a timetable exactly when he can resume the activity.

Preparing for change

"If we do something unexpected, or we don't follow her routine, Suresh throws a major tantrum."

Making sense of it

- Many children with Asperger syndrome seem to need routines. They may build these up for themselves. They may become 'hooked' on a part of their everyday routine.
- Changes to routines can cause major problems. It is as if the person is frightened by the uncertainty of not being able to predict what comes next.
- Unexpected events can cause the same problems. However, some people with Asperger syndrome seem to accept really major changes such as a new house or a foreign holiday, while not being able to cope with smaller scale changes.

Things to try

- Go along with Suresh's need for routines. Build a timetable which clearly shows the routine. For example:
  a Choose a particular word, picture, line drawing or symbol to go with each part of the daily routine. Mount these on separate cards which can be put in a photograph album.
  b Get Suresh into the habit of taking out the card at the start of the activity and putting it away at the end. Help her to understand the link between a particular card and the activity it stands for.
  c Once she seems to understand the link between the cards and the activities, start to arrange the pictures to show the order of the routine for the next half day. You may be able to build up to a whole day.
  d Before you start an activity, go and get the card. Point out what you are going to do and what will be happening next.
  e Once Suresh is used to the timetable, you may be able to introduce one or two changes of activity. Point these out to her well ahead of their happening. The fact that she gets advance warning of what's going to happen, and what will happen afterwards, may help her to cope with change. This is where it is important that the cards represent separate activities, so that the new activity cards can be inserted into the familiar routine.
- Some changes may be difficult for Suresh to understand in advance, particularly if the change involves a new place or new people. Video recordings or photographs can be used to prepare her.
- It may be helpful for Suresh to take something that is familiar into the new situation, in the same way that young children use a cuddly blanket or a soft toy.
- Use very simple, precise language, that will explain what is happening. Tell Suresh what will happen **after** the unexpected event.

Sensory/motor difficulties

"When Aaron goes into the dining room at school or a busy, noisy cafe, he runs into a corner, puts his fingers in his ears and rocks to and fro: he will not listen and continuously talks over me."

Making sense of it
- Unusual reactions or over-sensitivity to specific noises are quite common in people with Asperger syndrome.
- Some may be irritated and distracted by noises occurring in the environment, eg the lawn being mowed, an aeroplane passing overhead, a light buzzing faintly in the classroom.
- Some people with Asperger syndrome place their fingers over their ears. Some fiddle with equipment on the desk. Some interrupt frequently. Some make humming noises. These may be methods of 'tuning out' the sound which is disturbing them.
- Some will be very distractible and find it difficult to pay attention when the noises which distress them are nearby. They may actually find the noises painful or very intrusive.

Things to try
- Try to cut down as many sources of extraneous noise as possible – or deal with specific sources of noise (eg chair legs which have lost their rubber tips and which squeal on the floor).
- Put a table a little further away from the others, with one or two supportive and understanding peers to eat lunch with Aaron.
- Use what is termed a 'Social Story' (see **Further Reading – p49**) to show what is going to happen, how long lunch will last, to explain that the noise occurs naturally and not to annoy/hurt Aaron, and what will happen as soon as lunch is over. Follow up lunch with a favourite activity to encourage Aaron to cope.
- There are always going to be certain sounds and noises in the environment which may upset Aaron. It will be necessary to **gradually** expose him to these stimuli to increase his tolerance and ability to cope appropriately when they occur. (See **Imagination/Rigidity – Phobias – p27**).

31

Inappropriate reactions to touch, or misinterpretation of physical contact

"Alison likes people and is very much part of the class, but if someone accidentally bumps into her, touches her while talking to her, or gives her a hug, she will scream and even lash out."

Making sense of it

- People with Asperger syndrome often display a heightened, over exaggerated response to touch. They may dislike the feeling of certain types of touch in particular situations. When touched by another person in an unpredictable way the individual shows a flight or fright response.
- People with Asperger syndrome may like the person who has hugged them, but not like the sudden physical contact.
- Some like physical contact if it is on their terms, however have difficulty coping with it when approached by other people.
- It can also be difficult for a youngster with Asperger syndrome to make sense of what the touch is intended to 'mean'. She may not recognise that the other person is trying to be friendly or just get her attention.

Things to try

- Always try to approach Alison from the front and give a clear verbal warning of what is going to happen, eg "Alison, that work was brilliant, give me a high five".
- With Alison and her parent's permission talk to the class about Alison's difficulties with touch and encourage them to show her tolerance and understanding. Discuss ideas for ways they can respond when she reacts this way.
- Always 'de-brief' Alison after an incident. Use simple, clear language. Explain why the situation occurred and discuss what Alison could have done, maybe modelling a more appropriate reaction.
- Teach Alison some 'calming' strategies to help her cope with an incident. These could be some relaxation/breathing exercises or a set phrase used to relieve stress or anxiety.
- Role model situations and practise more appropriate responses with Alison to help her cope with unexpected contact.
- Allow Alison to sit at the end of a table, or by the edge of the group on the floor – she may need her own space to feel comfortable. During assembly let her sit at the end of a row, near the front or back of the hall.
- In some school settings it may be possible to offer sessions which involve massage and aromatherapy. The areas massaged should be the extremities which feel most comfortable to Alison. This activity should take place with people Alison feels safe and comfortable with and in accordance with child protection procedures.

Hypersensitivity to visual stimuli

"Emily closes her eyes when she walks into a 'busy' classroom. She doesn't seem able to choose what to look at and can't cope with everything."

Making sense of it
- Some people with Asperger syndrome may stare through people and avoid looking them in the eye.
- They may appear clumsy and ungainly, often seeming hesitant about negotiating steps and kerbs etc. They often pay no attention to peers but will locate a tiny scrap on the floor and give it most careful and prolonged inspection or attention. They may find it hard to determine which piece of visual information is relevant, and rarely see the 'bigger picture'.
- Some people with Asperger syndrome report words on blackboards as merging together to become a meaningless jumble.
- People with Asperger syndrome might be unable to tolerate bright, flickering lights or sunlight and may be considerably calmer when in a darkened room. Certain light can even be painful.

Things to try
- Provide Emily with a 'distraction free' work area. This might mean turning her desk so that it faces a blank wall to limit visual stimuli. It will be important for this work area only to be used when Emily is expected to be doing work on her own. There will be other times where she should be part of the group.
- Limit the visual distraction in the environment by making it as structured as possible. Work areas, worksheets, even display spaces where possible, should not involve 'cluttered' visual information.
- Worksheets are likely to require differentiating so that they are uncluttered, but provide clear visual information, such as: where to start, where to finish, where to put the answers etc.
- In situations where Emily is likely to be overloaded by the amount of visual stimuli, suggest that she focuses on particular things. This can be introduced with a video of a situation pointing out what it is relevant and important to attend to.
- Talk to Emily about her difficulties coping with visual stimuli. This may give you an insight into 'how it is for her' and coping strategies may result from this discussion.
- If Emily has difficulty giving eye contact, respect this. However, teach her socially acceptable ways of giving minimal or no eye contact. For example, if Emily is being addressed by a teacher it would be more appropriate for her to glance occasionally at the teacher and look down than it would be to stare over the teacher's shoulder or up in the air.

Emotional difficulties

Developing self control

"Why does Wesley hit out when there doesn't seem to be any reason?"

Making sense of it

- Most people with Asperger syndrome have problems in understanding the motives and intentions of others. They find coping with other people, particularly in less structured situations, very stressful indeed. On occasions this tension can 'spill out' in the form of frustrated outbursts.
- The emotional development of children with Asperger syndrome tends to proceed at a slower pace. They will often react in a way which is typical of much younger children.
- Children with Asperger syndrome are less motivated by what other people think of them and may not understand how their behaviour looks (or feels) from someone else's perspective. This may make them less likely to inhibit their own behaviour.
- Children like Wesley often want friends but have great difficulty in making or sustaining relationships. Angry outbursts are sometimes a reaction to the frustrations and disappointments they experience in this area.
- Some children with Asperger syndrome will dwell on things that have happened, or re-live incidents that may have taken place some time ago. They may become fixated on real or imagined wrongs to them – this may then spill out as quite an intense 'delayed reaction'.

Things to try

- It may be easier to modify aspects of the environment than to change Wesley's basic style of thinking and feeling. Look for triggers and see if any of these can be avoided or modified. This may mean working with other children, using approaches such as Circles of Friends (see **Further Reading – p49**).
- Wesley will need help to recognise when he is getting upset. He may benefit from self calming strategies or simply require a routine for getting away from situations where a loss of self control seems likely. This will need to be rehearsed and when introduced into 'real-life' situations Wesley will need to be given cues. See **Social relationships – When friendships fail – p13.**

- It is important to de-brief Wesley after incidents. This should be separated from any sanction that is imposed so that the discussion can be kept calm, simple and factual. Focus on identifying the early stages of the incident and looking at ways in which the difficulty might have been resolved or avoided.
- Don't forget to offer incentives for self control (for days, half days or even half hours when an outburst **hasn't** occurred).

Anxiety

"David gets worked up about what's going to happen. He asks questions over and over again, and goes to pieces if things have to be changed."

Making sense of it

- Most children with Asperger syndrome find it difficult to predict what is going to happen.
- Some become highly dependent on routines and sameness for their emotional security.
- Some may ask questions repetitively just to make sure the answer is still the same or because hearing the answer makes them feel safe. (See **Communication – Repetitive questioning – p23**).
- Many children have difficulties recognising and expressing emotions and this can lead to anxiety.
- Most will have problems understanding other peoples expectations and motives due to their basic difficulty with empathy: social situations may be particularly difficult.
- Some may internalise their anxiety which results in self injurious behaviours, eg hand biting.
- Some children's anxiety is the result of fears which may have had their origins in a genuinely frightening experience, eg fire alarms. Fear that this experience may be repeated may come to dominate the child's life – even in situations which bear little resemblance to the original one.

Things to try

- As far as practical, try to provide a consistent daily routine. Children with Asperger syndrome benefit from predictability and stability in their environment.
- Make sure David is forewarned of any changes in his expected routine. Prepare him thoroughly in advance of special activities or known changes. It may be necessary to back up any verbal explanations with visual or printed material in case he needs to reassure himself (or didn't take in your explanation).
- Irrational fears usually respond to gradual de-sensitisation – give the child the chance to encounter what they are frightened of – but in a controlled setting where the child feels in charge and their exposure to what frightens them is 'diluted' (eg a tape of the fire bell, played at low volume; a video of a dog etc). See **Imagination/Rigidity – Phobias – p27.**
- Look at the section on **Social Relationships** for ideas about helping David make sense of other people and common social situations.
- Novel activities may need very careful introduction. Try to be as concrete as possible in describing them and check the child's understanding (eg a video of what happens on a residential trip may be easier for the child to take in). You may find the child is better at coping with huge changes than minor alterations to familiar routines.
- Teach strategies for relieving or controlling anxiety. Some commercially available stress-relief toys can be helpful, as can various relaxation routines.

Frustration and mood swings

"John can be fine one minute, happily getting on with life. Then suddenly everything falls apart and he's really uptight."

Making sense of it

- Some children with Asperger syndrome show greater than average levels of frustration because of their inability to adequately express their feelings or make sense of everyday social situations.
- Some are susceptible to fluctuating mood swings – these could be connected to obsessional thoughts or behaviours or may be due to external sensory experiences, such as noise or light.
- Some children seem to follow a cyclical pattern which determines their moods.
- Many children with Asperger syndrome will not easily develop the social awareness which inhibit most people's behaviour and may show their frustration if made to wait or defer their wishes.

Things to try

- Try to develop John's emotional vocabulary. Interpret how you think he is feeling and give the feeling a name. John will gradually build a memory store of emotional experiences and will develop a more general concept of what leads to each emotion and what it feels like.
- If John is highly obsessional try to set aside times during the day when he can talk about or practise his obsession. Obsessions and routines are often driven by anxiety. To try to eradicate them will inevitably lead to greater frustration.
- Check whether John's mood swings are coinciding with especially sunnier days or higher levels of noise. If so changing where he sits in class may help or tinted glasses could be tried to prevent light sensitivity.
- If the mood swings seem to be cyclical and have no apparent external cause the child may need medical help. The child could be suffering from depression, which is not uncommon in children with a degree of self awareness. (See **Depression – p40**).
- Give John advance warning of changes in his routine which are likely to frustrate him. Prepare him for times when he must wait or, for example, be second in line rather than first, and offer praise if he copes. Gradually increase the occasions when he has to defer his wishes.
- Don't expect John to spontaneously let you know how he is feeling. Even if he has this level of self awareness he may not appreciate that you might be interested or concerned.
- Make sure that there is someone who has responsibility for over-seeing John's well-being – and make sure John knows who he can turn to.

Self awareness

"James seems increasingly conscious that he is different from other people and keeps asking why he is different."

Making sense of it

- Children with Asperger syndrome seem to reach a point of development where they are aware that they are different from others. This often follows a period of time where they have seen differences between themselves and others, but played down or blamed others for the differences. This realisation of 'difference' occurs at different times for different children. For a few it occurs while they are still at Primary School. However, for the majority it occurs during adolescence and while they are attending Secondary School.

- The decision about whether or not the child should be told of their condition **must** be left to the child's parents. However, you may want to raise this possibility with the parents if you have reason to believe this is becoming an issue.

- If a child is to be told you may want to seek advice from other professionals about the best way of preparing and supporting the child.

Things to try

If James is not aware that he has Asperger syndrome

- Talk to James' class, while he is there, about individual differences and how we can all support each other.

- Consider 'counselling' sessions with a favourite adult where James is encouraged to discuss anything that is bothering him.

If James is aware that he has Asperger syndrome

- Offer opportunities on a frequent basis for discussing the implications of Asperger syndrome with someone who he trusts (see **Further Reading** for details of 'Pictures of me' – **p49**).

- Offer opportunities to meet and discuss Asperger syndrome with others who also have Asperger syndrome.

- Provide access to materials written by others with Asperger syndrome and appropriate professionals.

- Offer an opportunity to correspond with others with Asperger syndrome as Pen Pals. (see **Further Reading – p49**).

Depression

"Umar has bouts of feeling really down."

Making sense of it

■ Many children with Asperger syndrome repeatedly experience failure or rejection in social situations. What others seem to do naturally requires great effort on their part – and even then, their attempts to 'read' others may not be successful.

■ The management of some children with Asperger syndrome can be very time consuming and demanding. Their relationship with adults in school may be overshadowed by these difficulties.

■ Children with Asperger syndrome have difficulty understanding how others think and feel. They often put a great deal of effort into this and become upset when they do not read others correctly.

■ Some people with Asperger syndrome become aware that they are different. They become depressed about this as they would like to be like others.

Things to try

■ Ensure that someone has responsibility for actively monitoring Umar's well being and providing opportunities for him to discuss his feelings. This may need to start at the very basic level of developing a 'vocabulary' of feelings.

■ Don't expect Umar to actively seek out an adult so that he can talk about how he's doing. He may not be aware of his own state or realise that it could be helpful to talk to someone.

■ Try to involve him in monitoring himself – trying to identify good and bad days and trying to see what has contributed to any pattern that emerges.

■ Try to develop a set of 'pick me up' strategies which can be used when he's feeling low.

■ Be alert to signs of more serious difficulty. Watch out for signs of deterioration in attentiveness, and organisation, reduced stress threshold and self isolation. If need be, discuss with his parents and take steps to involve outside help. Umar's parents will need to discuss the situation with their GP.

Work skills

Motivation

"Jason would write whole books on space flight if we asked him to – but he just won't do a thing about Roman Britain."

Making sense of it
- A very typical feature of Asperger syndrome is an intense interest in one specific (and often very narrow) topic – and limited interest in almost anything else.
- The 'social' sources of motivation that work with many youngsters don't seem to operate as strongly with pupils with Asperger syndrome: they may not be as interested in 'pleasing people' or modelling themselves on a favourite adult.
- Limitations of imagination may make long term incentives and considerations (such as exam results, career prospects etc) ineffective.
- Youngsters with Asperger syndrome (particularly in adolescence) may be so pre-occupied with their difficulties and their feelings about these problems that they have little spare 'capacity' to focus on work.

Things to try
- If Jason is relatively young it may be possible to address certain areas of the curriculum through his interests in space. Scope for this strategy tends to reduce as children progress through school.
- It is always worth trying to use any obsessive interest as a source of reward and motivation, eg "**if** you complete this work by 10.30, **then** you get 10 minutes on your space project".
- Expectations about quantity and quality of work output need to be explicit and detailed. It is better to use very short term targets to begin with, gradually extending their duration.
- External incentives of some kind are likely to be helpful. However, remember that it is better to reward 'little and often' and take care when choosing the reward. It is always better to ask the child for ideas about possible rewards/incentives. The usual range of classroom rewards may not be effective.
- Try to use visual systems to let Jason know how well he's doing – and how close he is to getting his chosen reward. This is especially important once he has to cope with significant delays.

Personal organisation

"Chris has great difficulty getting from A to B and when he gets there he can never get the right things out of his bag for the lesson."

Making sense of it

- Children with Asperger syndrome often seem to have great difficulty with personal organisation. They can appear to be overloaded and confused by having to simultaneously cope with language, perceptual stimulation and social demands. (This can happen to all of us in certain circumstances – but people with Asperger syndrome seem to have a much lower threshold.)
- The youngster with Asperger syndrome may also not see the point of making the extra effort needed for personal organisation – the motive to please people or get work finished or to master particular skills may be poorly developed.
- These organisational problems show themselves at a number of different levels:
    - knowing where to stand in open spaces and how to get from A to B
    - knowing where to put answers on worksheets or how to organise drawings and text on a blank page
    - having the right materials for the right lessons
    - knowing what to bring from home and take home on a given day.

Things to try

- Give Chris a map for getting around the school.
- Provide support for getting around the school, preferably a peer.
- Make a list of what is needed for each lesson which is readily accessible. Prompt its use if necessary.
- Mark the beginning of work with a sign, eg a green traffic light, and similarly the end.
- Enlarge worksheets and make it very clear where the answers should go by marking this area with clear boundaries or colours.
- Mark areas to sit or stand in open spaces with a PE hoop, a carpet square, a cushion to sit on, etc.
- Develop a written or symbol timetable to go home in Chris' school bag. (See **Over-dependency – p44**). The timetable should provide him with what he needs to give to his parents and what he needs to bring to school the next day.

Concentration and the learning environment

"Kirsty's all over the place. She just doesn't seem to be able to settle down and focus on what she should be doing."

Making sense of it

- People with Asperger syndrome may be capable of good concentration – but what they choose to concentrate on can be very idiosyncratic.
- Youngsters with Asperger syndrome may have difficulty picking out what they should focus on – especially if they haven't listened to, or understood, the instructions.
- They may be particularly vulnerable to distractions from external sources and seem to have difficulty in filtering out irrelevant stimuli (particularly sounds and visual information).
- Their thoughts and pre-occupations may also be experienced as very intrusive – often causing them distress.
- If they are finding school stressful, children with Asperger syndrome may actively withdraw into their own fantasy world.

Things to try

- A fundamental strategy for many youngsters like Kirsty is to provide high levels of structure. This works at a number of different levels.
- If practical, it can be extremely helpful to establish a separate 'work station' where independent work is to be completed. Ideally this needs to offer as few distractions as possible – away from 'traffic areas', facing a blank wall and possibly screened in some way (large cardboard boxes are useful!). Make sure all work materials are available and organised before the session starts. The aim is to build an association between this location and 'getting work done'.
- Visual prompts can be very helpful. They can be used to show Kirsty what activities are coming next (particularly useful if they are motivating to her). At a more detailed level they can show the steps in the particular task. Symbols or words can also be used to remind Kirsty of basic rules and expectations.
- External time limits (using a kitchen timer or similar) combined with very specific work assignments may help the child focus. If this can also be linked to incentives this may motivate them to make the effort needed to resist distractions.
- Tasks need to be very carefully and clearly structured. The steps need to be spelled out explicitly and the expected end product described in concrete detail.
- Be careful to be realistic about the pace of work and level of concentration you expect. If Kirsty is receiving any amount of 1:1 help this can be quite intense and demanding. She may not be able to keep up this pace through the whole day and will, at least, have produced some work during these 1:1 sessions.
- Depending on Kirsty's relationships with her classmates it can be useful to use a buddy system, with other children offering occasional reminders to concentrate (using some **agreed** prompt or codeword).

Over-dependency

"Michael won't do anything unless I'm sitting next to him telling him what to do – even things he can do really easily."

Making sense of it

- Many children with Asperger syndrome don't like change and get locked into patterns of doing things in the same way and with the same people.
- Sometimes the adult's presence seems to act as a type of physical prompt which, if removed, prevents the child from continuing, even if the task is very familiar. The adult can feel that a 'cardboard cut-out' would be just as effective.
- Some children do not have the social motivation to be independent and rarely take a pride in saying "Let me do it myself" as other children do.
- Many have poor self esteem and confidence and feel more secure when with an adult.
- Sometimes the supporting adult feels that they are only doing their job properly if they are with the child all the time and may inadvertently encourage the dependency.

Things to try

- As soon as Michael has learned a few skills set up a time each day when he can practice them independently. Make sure what you are demanding is well within his capabilities. The focus should be on developing Michael's independence rather than on the specific task.
- To help his understanding of what is expected make his independent work as structured as possible, eg sitting at a special table, tasks sequenced and clear indications of when to start and finish (See **Concentration and the learning environment – p43**).
- Praise Michael every time he successfully completes a task unsupported. Teach him a way of telling someone when he has finished, eg verbally, with a 'finished' card, or by putting away equipment.
- Encourage everyone who supports Michael at any time of the day to gradually increase the times when he is expected to manage alone. They should give him space but be ready to step in if needed.
- Make sure that Michael is helped to organise equipment and has understood and begun the task before reducing support. Initially the adult could shift their attention to providing help for another child nearby.
- Encourage Michael's peers to provide some of the support rather than the adult, eg taking him out to play, working on the computer. It may be necessary to guard against 'over-helpfulness'.

Problems with recording

"Jack has great difficulty writing. His writing is 'spidery' and gets worse if he has to think about what he is writing."

Making sense of it

- Many children with Asperger syndrome also have fine motor difficulties which make writing difficult for them.
- Some of these children still have to concentrate on the 'mechanics' of handwriting. If also asked to think about what they are writing down their handwriting may suffer.
- Some may be able to write well at the beginning of an activity but quickly become tired.
- Some demonstrate greater difficulties with handwriting if they are anxious (either about handwriting or something else).
- Some have difficulty with working to a time limit and find it difficult to finish a piece of work.

Things to try

- While it is important for Jack to develop handwriting skills this is not the only method of recording. Alternatives which can be explored are:
    computer
    tape recorder
    dictating
    cut and stick
    cloze procedure.
- It may be necessary to plan how Jack will be expected to record his work across the various lessons in any week. The aim is to ensure a balance of methods (and offer clarity and reassurance to staff). These expectations should be marked clearly on his timetable.
- Let Jack know how much he is expected to write. The student with Asperger syndrome has difficulty predicting what you are expecting from them.
- Recognise anxieties and, if possible, reduce pressure in these situations.
- Try to use markers of time passing such as sand timers, pieces of known music, timers etc. These will give Jack a visual or auditory prompt of time passing and the need to finish his writing in time.

Remembering

"Harjas is not able to tell me what he has done at school unless I ask him lots of questions. If I hit on the right thing then he tells me lots of things."

Making sense of it

- Some students with Asperger syndrome have difficulty accessing their memory. It is not that the memory is not there, they seem to have difficulty retrieving it. Often they seem to need a very precise and specific cue.
- Many have difficulty responding to open questions, eg "What did you do at school today?" but are able to answer questions with forced alternatives, eg "Did you go horse riding or swimming today?"

Things to try

- Try to provide Harjas with cues which help him retrieve information from memory. Organise the information and give him headings or 'key words' that will serve as reminders.
- Communicate carefully with home, perhaps through Harjas' home-school book or his homework diary. List key words which are likely to trigger the child's memory.
- Be aware of the difficulties with open questions and only use these when you feel Harjas will be able to retrieve the answer from his memory. At other times support him by asking questions which will cue him in, such as forced alternatives.
- If Harjas is expected to memorise specific information try to encourage him to **actively** process it. He may be helped by a number of techniques:
  - trying to build the information into a diagram or picture
  - help him to build personal links between new information or concepts and what he already knows. Try to personalise the information
  - teach strategies for remembering. Encourage rehearsal, web diagrams etc
  - when talking about experiences with the child emphasise their personal involvement and reactions to the activities.

Homework: to do or not to do

"Jenny only does the homework she feels like doing. She doesn't seem to care if she hasn't done it and is put into detention."

Making sense of it

- Some children with Asperger syndrome cannot cope with homework because it muddles up the boundary between home and school which confuses them.
- Most lack the usual social motivation to please parents or teachers.
- Many just cannot 'see the point' in homework even though they can verbalise why it should be completed, eg to gain better coursework marks.
- Some children with Asperger syndrome will try to give reasons for not producing homework. Their reason may have been valid on one occasion but they may continue to offer it each time, whether appropriate or not.
- Most will produce some homework, often on topics they find interesting, but may have difficulties meeting time limits due to poor personal organisation skills (see **Personal organisation – p42**).

Things to try

- Work with Jenny's parents. Keep them informed and look at ways for them to help motivate and organise her.
- Ensure that all staff give clear instructions which can be understood by parents as well as Jenny. She may not understand her own written instructions once out of the classroom context. A dictaphone may be useful (see **Problems with recording – p45**).
- A meeting to set up a homework policy may be helpful, including parents, ancillary support and Jenny. She may benefit from seeing and hearing everyone discuss the issues and will then be under no illusion as to who knows what.
- Devise a whole staff approach to the problem. Consistency is essential. Avoid one teacher issuing a detention while another is ignoring the problem. Jenny will either be totally confused or may take advantage of the inconsistency.
- Detention is unlikely to be effective and may exacerbate the problem. Lunchtime detentions remove Jenny from opportunities to socialise which she needs but which she can find challenging.
- Try to think of something motivating for Jenny to work towards. Talk to her to see what she would find motivating. It may be something unusual but easily provided. Remember to continue to offer social praise as well.

Further reading

Circles of friends

This approach involves working directly with the youngster and a small number of his or her classmates. The circle of friends acts as a practical, problem solving group and as a source of emotional support. More details of the technique is provided in:

> Barratt P, Joy H, Potter M, Thomas G and Whitaker P (1998) 'Children with autism and peer group support'. *British Journal of Special Education* Vol 25 No 2, pp 1-16.

This article also refers to other authors who describe the background to this general approach and offer advice about its use to support inclusion in general.

Friends for me

This curriculum provides a social skills lessons that is designed to help children and youth with Asperger syndrome make friends. Contact:

> Moore, S. M. (2002). *Friends for Me: A social skills program for children and youth with Asperger Syndrome.* Shawnee Mission, KS: AAPC.

Pen pals

Youngsters with Asperger Syndrome can be put in touch with each other via the Asperger Syndrome Coalition of the United States or the *Morning News.* For information contact:

ASC-US	Jenison Public Schools
PO Box 351268	2140 Bauer Road
Jacksonville	Jenison
FL 32235-1265	M1 49428

Pictures of me

This is a very specific example of the 'Social Story' method devised by Carol Gray. With the support of a trusted adult the youngster is involved in collaboratively writing and illustrating a booklet about him or herself. Through a carefully thought out sequence the youngster is helped to look at his or her personality and talents – and then at the difficulties and needs which arise as a result of Asperger syndrome.

An outline of the approach is provided in:

> Gray C. (1997, Winter) 'Pictures of me – introducing students with Asperger syndrome to their talents, personality and diagnosis' *Communication,* pp 22-24.

Social use of language programme

This programme is aimed at enhancing the social communication of children of primary and secondary age who have special educational needs – rather than Asperger syndrome specifically. It offers an assessment and record keeping framework. It also includes teaching activities for specific interactive skills (including awareness of self and others) and suggestions for practising skills in social contexts). Details are as follows:

Rinaldi W (1992) *Social use of Language Programme* NFER-Nelson

Social stories

This is an approach developed by Carol Gray. It involves writing an individualised story which describes a specific social situation in terms of the relevant social cues and responses. Carol Gray provides guidance about the relative proportions of descriptive (as opposed to prescriptive) sentences to be used and recommends mentioning other people's perspectives as well.

A description of the technique and examples of its use can be found in:

Swaggart B L, et al (1995) 'Using social stories to teach social and behavioural skills to children with autism' *Focus on Autistic Behaviour* Vol 10 No 1, pp1-14.

Useful addresses

THE ASPERGER SYNDROME COALITION OF THE UNITED STATES (ASC-US)

Headquarters

PO Box 351268

Jacksonville, FL 32235-1265

Switchboard: 764-4-ASPRGR

Website: www.asperger.org

THE AUTISM SOCIETY OF AMERICA (ASA)

Headquarters

7910 Woodmont Avenue, Suite 200

Bethesda, MD 20814-3067

Switchboard: 301 657 0881

Website: www.autism-society.org

MAAP SERVICES INC.

Headquarters

PO Box 524

Crown Point, IN 46308

Switchboard: 219 662 1311

Website: www.maapservices.org

THE NATIONAL AUTISTIC SOCIETY

Headquarters

393 City Road, London EC1V 1NE

Switchboard: 0171 833 2299

Fax: 0171 833 9666

Useful addresses